T0418297

BE THE **Change!** POLITICAL PARTICIPATION IN YOUR COMMUNITY™

WORKING WITH THE COMMUNITY

IN A POLITICAL CAMPAIGN

Melissa Banigan

New York

Published in 2020 by The Rosen Publishing Group, Inc.
29 East 21st Street, New York, NY 10010

Copyright © 2020 by The Rosen Publishing Group, Inc.

First Edition

All rights reserved. No part of this book may be reproduced in any form
without permission in writing from the publisher, except by a reviewer.

Cataloging-in-Publication Data

Names: Banigan, Melissa, author.
Title: Working with the community in a political campaign / Melissa Banigan.
Description: New York : Rosen Publishing, 2020 | Series: Be the change!
: political participation in your community | Includes bibliographical
references and index. | Audience: Grade 7 to 12.
Identifiers: ISBN 9781725340909 (library bound) | ISBN 9781725340893 (pbk.)
Subjects: LCSH: Political campaigns—United States—Juvenile literature. | Campaign
management—United States—Juvenile literature. | Political participation—
United States—Juvenile literature. | Communities—Juvenile literature.
Classification: LCC JK2281.B34 2020 | DDC 324.7'20973—dc23

Manufactured in the United States of America

CONTENTS

INTRODUCTION

In early 1860, Republican presidential candidate Abraham Lincoln was so unknown to potential voters that even he didn't think he'd get elected. One evening, however, while giving a speech in Connecticut against slavery, he saw hundreds of enthusiastic young men in the audience and thought that maybe, just maybe, he had a fighting chance.

The men were part of a volunteer brigade of Republicans called the Wide Awakes. Wanting nothing more than to see a fellow Republican elected president—particularly one who stood against slavery—thousands of Wide Awakes flocked to rallies, speeches, picnics, and other events. They even started escorting Lincoln (and other Republicans) wherever he went. According to historian Bruce Chadwick, who authored a book about Lincoln's campaign, each of the passionate young men "felt he belonged to a group … For the Wide Awakes, the Lincoln campaign was a crusade, not just an election."

Recognizing the collective power of the volunteer brigade, Lincoln encouraged the Wide Awakes to continue their volunteer efforts. Their efforts paid off—at a single event in New York, more than nineteen thousand members of the group showed up, and by Election Day there were a whopping five hundred thousand members. While this might not seem like a

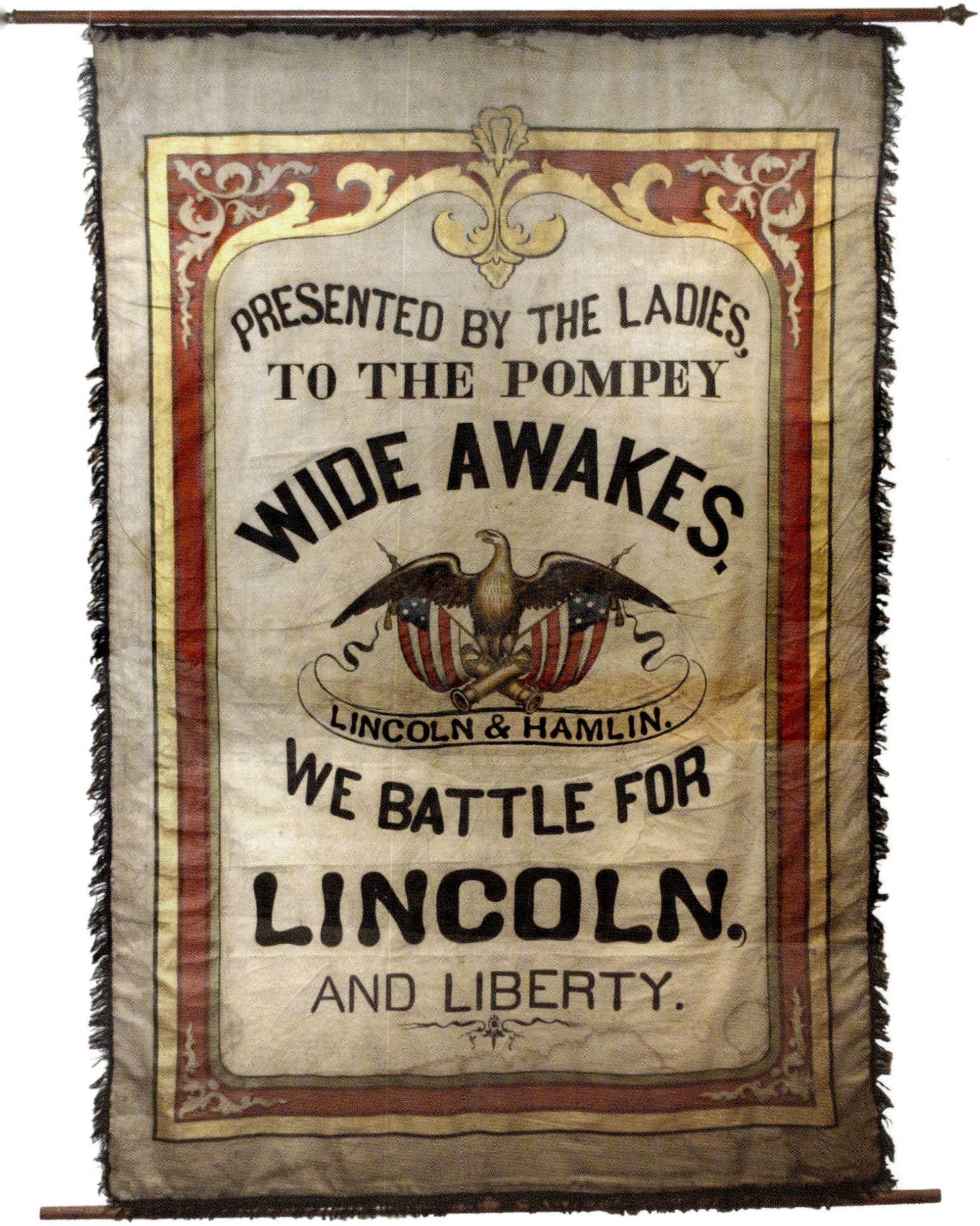

PRESENTED BY THE LADIES,
TO THE POMPEY
WIDE AWAKES.

LINCOLN & HAMLIN.

WE BATTLE FOR
LINCOLN.
AND LIBERTY.

The Wide Awakes, a volunteer brigade of young men, helped Abraham Lincoln get elected president of the United States.

large number today, it's important to keep in mind that in 1860, half a million people amounted to about one-sixtieth of the American population. Today, that would translate to more than five million members of the Wide Awakes!

One of the largest archives in American History, the Gilder Lehrman Collection, stated that the "Wide Awakes are credited with helping Abraham Lincoln win the nomination for President of the United States." They did this by enthusiastically showing up, spreading the word that Lincoln was a great candidate, and making communities feel that they had a large stake in the election.

There are two big lessons to be learned from the Wide Awakes: political candidates are only as powerful as the contingents of volunteers fighting to help them win elections; and communities must be engaged with a campaign and inspired to vote.

In some ways, Lincoln had it pretty easy—the Wide Awakes had not only organized independently of his campaign, but they also convinced communities in many cities to head to the voting polls. This meant that all Lincoln had to do was provide them with a little encouragement.

Most candidates, however, don't have it so easy. Usually, passionate volunteers like the Wide Awakes don't just show up on their own, ready to inspire people to vote. Campaigns need to recruit, train, and dispatch volunteers into local communities to engage with potential voters.

Above all else, political campaigns must focus on delivering results for communities. In 1860, the young men involved with the Wide Awakes envisioned a country where all people were free from the shackles of slavery. They felt strongly that Abraham Lincoln was the person to get the job done. And they were correct. In 1863, President Lincoln issued an executive order called the Emancipation Proclamation, which promised to end slavery across the United States. Two years later, after the Civil War ended, the Thirteenth Amendment to the United States Constitution forever abolished slavery in America.

Not every politician has as big a job as ending slavery, but all communities have needs. The best political campaigns—and the campaigns that win elections—strive to meet those needs.

CHAPTER ONE

IT'S NOT JUST ABOUT THE CANDIDATE

Just a few months before the release of Christopher Nolan's second *Batman* movie, a website was launched to promote an ad campaign for the film's fictional political candidate, Harvey Dent. Dent—or rather, an actor playing Dent—also called people who had registered their phone numbers with the site. He said:

> We all know what's wrong with Gotham. Crime is out of control, and instead of protecting our streets, too many cops have become criminals themselves. This is why my mission has been to stamp out police corruption. And this is why I'm considering a run for District Attorney. But I can't do it alone. I need to know if you, the people of Gotham, want change. Do you want a Gotham free from the grip of criminals and the corrupt? Are you ready to join a crusade to take back our city?

The ad campaign was meant to convince people to see the new *Batman* movie rather than actually get them to vote for a fictional character, but the message tapped into the single most important element of a political campaign: teamwork. "I can't do it alone," said Dent, and indeed, political candidates are only as strong as the communities that support their campaigns and the electorates (eligible people allowed to vote) who vote them into office.

WON'T YOU BE MY NEIGHBOR?

Fred Rogers—who developed and starred in the television show *Mister Rogers' Neighborhood*—famously asked his audience, "Won't you be my neighbor?" His show explored relationships with many of the people who make up a community—his local mail carrier, firefighter, phone operator, and chef, for example. He'd invite them into his television house, ask them about their lives, and speak with them about their ideas. One of the characters on his show, Mayor Maggie, even spoke with other characters in sign language.

In *Mister Rogers' Neighborhood*, learning how to communicate well with others was the best way to be a good neighbor. Political campaigns can learn a lot from the lessons taught in the show. After all, for a political campaign to help a candidate win an election, it's important to not

Political candidates should ask the same question Mr. Rogers asked on his show, *Mister Rogers' Neighborhood*: "Won't you be my neighbor?"

only know who lives within the communities, but what makes them tick.

WHAT IS A CENSUS?

The US Census is important—in fact, the country's democracy is based on it! In 1790, Thomas Jefferson, James Madison, and other founders of the newly formed United States developed a plan that would allow people to have more power than the government. But to give people this power, the country first needed to count every single individual and know where all those people lived. Based on the results of this process—called a census—each community received a certain number of politicians to represent them in Congress.

Figuring out how many people are in the United States was deemed so important that the census was even written into the US Constitution. After all, the Constitution protected all people living in the United States, no matter where they were from. Not only did the Constitution protect all people, but it presented a radical idea that all people must be equally represented by the government—even if they couldn't vote.

The Constitution hasn't been without its faults. In the eighteenth century, slaves were counted as only three-fifths of a person. After the Civil War, this was rectified by writing a new amendment (the Fourteenth Amendment) to the Constitution that stated—once and for all—that all people must be counted equally.

Taking place every ten years, the census counts every single person living in the United States, including US citizens, undocumented immigrants, and everyone in between. It helps to show how and where populations are changing over time. In addition to determining how many votes each state will have, the census helps figure out how much federal and state funding to divide appropriately based on population.

Political candidates at national and state levels need to study current census information to understand their communities.

APPLES AND ORANGES: LEARNING WHICH ISSUES ARE REALLY IMPORTANT

Most people like eating fruit. Imagine there are two bowls: one is filled with apples, the other with oranges. Chances are that most people have a preference for one of these types of fruit over the other. After all, each of them has a different taste and texture. Even the way they're eaten is different: one must be peeled while the other can be bitten into.

Political issues are sort of like big bowls of fruit. For

Taking time to learn the political preferences of voters can make all the difference at the polls on Election Day.

example, most people would agree that they want good health care. But some people would prefer to have the government pay for every single person to have the same quality of health care, while other people prefer to have choices for health care, even if that means they have to pay for some of it out of their own pocket.

During a political campaign, it's not enough to simply tell potential voters that a candidate likes fruit. Instead, they must head out into the community to learn which type of fruit—or which particular issues—are most important to voters. This is often done two ways: through polling or with focus groups.

A poll is simply a group of questions asked of a random group of people. For example, a poll might ask 300 out of 1,200 students at a local high school whether they prefer apples or oranges, soft or hard fruit, or fruit that needs to be peeled or bitten into. Asking 300 students saves a lot of time—it would take a lot longer to ask 1,200 students and then run through the polling results—but it also offers a good representation of the entire student population.

Focus groups are similar in that small groups of people are collected to discuss various issues. In one room, for example, a focus group might be discussing the benefits of citrus fruit over apples, while in another room a different focus group might talk about how apple trees are good for the environment. These groups give political campaigns invaluable information: for example, a campaign might learn that although people like oranges better than apples, they don't like how most orange groves use pesticides, and therefore, they buy more apples.

COUNTING IMMIGRANTS, HOMELESS PEOPLE, AND OTHER UNDERSERVED PEOPLE

You don't have to be a US citizen to be counted in the US Census. There are millions of undocumented immigrants, noncitizen legal residents, and noncitizen long-term visitors who live in the United States and are supposed to be included in the count. This is very important, as the US Constitution protects all people within the country, whether or not they are from the United States. Sadly, many of these people aren't counted in the census. Some undocumented immigrants, for example, avoid answering census questions for fear of being deported.

It's not just immigrants who sometimes aren't counted—many homeless people are also left out. The US Census Bureau tries to count every single American household by sending materials to all known

Undocumented immigrants, noncitizen legal residents, noncitizen long-term visitors, and people who are homeless in the United States should all be counted in the census.

(CONTINUED ON THE NEXT PAGE)

(CONTINUED FROM THE PREVIOUS PAGE)

addresses where people live. Yet some people and families don't have shelter, or they live in cars, in rural areas, or in other situations that aren't easy for the Census Bureau to locate.

In 2020, the US Census Bureau will urge people to respond to census questions using a form on the internet. Although this is a great idea in theory, it also means that people without access to the internet—particularly homeless people or individuals and families who can't afford it—won't be counted.

There is a big danger in not counting all people who live in the United States. Undercounting undocumented immigrants or homeless people means their concerns won't be taken into account when it comes to providing federal funding to states, cities, and towns. Many programs that help undocumented immigrants and homeless populations receive funding based on information collected from the census.

To ensure that every voice is counted, people can write to their representatives in Congress to demand a more accurate census, or they can join groups that work on "Get Out the Count" campaigns, such as the Census Project.

In short, it's not enough to know that a voter base wants good health care or quality schools. Candidates also need to know why these issues are important to voters and what kind of health care or schools they want.

DON'T FORGET THE VOTERS

In a democracy, voting is the most fundamental and important form of civic engagement. Yet by international standards, the United States has one of the lowest voter turnouts: according to the International Institute for Democracy and Electoral Assistance, only 57.7 percent of registered voters vote. Canada isn't too far behind, with only 68.28 percent of registered voters heading to the polls.

Whether they vote or not, all potential voters are members of communities. If a campaign pays attention only to people who typically vote, then there's not much incentive for people who usually don't vote to head to the polls.

THE "GOVERNATOR" WAS JUST LIKE EVERYONE ELSE

Austrian-born Arnold Schwarzenegger seemed like an unlikely candidate to run for the seat of California's governor. Yet this actor and former bodybuilder champion not only ran for office, he served as a Republican governor for over seven years! How did he do it? For starters, he used his popularity as an actor to appeal to voters.

Schwarzenegger was just wrapping up a promotional tour for his movie *Terminator 3* when he announced that he was running for office. Immediately, the media nicknamed him the "Governator," a riff on his character, the "Terminator." Schwarzenegger milked his fame by using many lines from his movies along the campaign trail. "I'll be back," he told an audience after a press conference, which was a line from the *Terminator* movies.

Of course, not everyone who heads into office is famous, but it always helps to find ways to be relatable. On the campaign trail, Schwarzenegger often talked about how he was just like other Californians. Before he became a famous actor, he told potential voters that he had started out with very little but had pulled himself up by his bootstraps. In short, Schwarzenegger appealed to voters by showing that he was just like your average, hardworking American. After winning the election, he said, "Everything I have is because of California. I came here with absolutely nothing, and California has given me absolutely everything."

President Barack Obama knew how to reach young voters via social media, but it was really his campaign strategy and messaging that inspired youth to head to the polls.

SOCIAL MEDIA FOR THE WIN

For decades, young people in the United States between the ages of eighteen and twenty-five were underrepresented in the polls. In 2008, however, the youth vote tripled and even quadrupled compared to the 2000 and 2004 elections. Why did so many young people flock to the polls? Two words: *social media.*

Barack Obama was a relatively unknown Democratic senator from Illinois, yet he won the highest office of the land by winning the youth vote. The first presidential candidate to really understand social media, Obama was attached at the hip to his BlackBerry, a device which was, at least back then, just as cool as the iPhone later became. In short, Obama's understanding of technology set him apart from other candidates who seemed to live almost in the technological dark ages.

Yet according to an article in the journal *Ethnicity & Disease*, Obama's win wasn't due to his own use of social media, but rather because of his campaign's extensive use of social networking sites, websites, and mobile devices to inspire youth who lived in hard-to-reach areas. Despite all of the dangers of social media (including bullying), when used wisely, it's proven to help swing elections by inspiring young voters who otherwise might not vote.

CHAPTER TWO

HOW TO RECRUIT VOLUNTEERS FOR A POLITICAL CAMPAIGN

Volunteers are like spines in that they support the entire body of a political campaign. Therefore, recruiting volunteers is really important. Sometimes, finding people to passionately support a campaign is as easy as asking members of the community to sign up, but other times, it takes a little more work.

FIND CAMPAIGN MANAGERS WITH UNIQUE TALENTS

Before going out to find volunteers, a political campaign must have at least a handful of key people to make the campaign's wheels start moving. Just as workplaces have managers and schools have principals, political campaigns need people to manage them. The job of campaign manager isn't easy. The person in this role needs to keep the campaign, volunteers, and all other people involved with the campaign motivated. A multifaceted job, campaign management includes

A great campaign manager works hard and often puts in long hours to ensure that all parts of a campaign run smoothly.

hiring staff, creating a budget, and overseeing the day-to-day operations of the campaign.

Campaign managers work long hours and need to put in a lot of elbow grease to get the job done (the job, of course, of getting their candidate elected to office!). A great campaign manager is typically visible to the public eye and, just like candidates, brings a unique style of leadership to the campaign.

A CAMPAIGN MANAGER WHO HELPS CANDIDATES CONTROL THEIR MESSAGES

Steve Schmidt is a communications strategist and political campaign manager who has worked on many Republican campaigns, including those of California governor Arnold Schwarzenegger, Arizona senator John McCain, and President George W. Bush. He's known for helping candidates master delivering strong messages. According to an article in *Newsweek* by Holly Bailey, "Schmidt's signature practice is to pick a simple message and repeat it day after day until it begins to sink in with the public."

Having too many messages means that an audience might miss the main messages. Therefore, Schmidt's

George W. Bush benefited from the wisdom of communications strategist Steve Schmidt, a skilled political campaign manager who has worked with a number of high-profile Republicans.

method of creating, sticking to, and repeating clear messages is key to drilling those ideas into the heads of potential voters … and volunteers inspired to join the campaign!

DEFYING STEREOTYPES TO INCREASE DIVERSITY IN POLITICS

In the past, campaign management was a profession traditionally occupied by men. Yet while women are unrepresented in politics, more women than ever are becoming campaign managers. In 2018, ABC News reported that women were running for office "in historic and never-before-seen numbers." Some of those campaigns were managed by women.

In her 2015 book, *Navigating Gendered Terrain: Stereotypes and Strategy in Political Campaigns*, political scientist Kelly Dittmar wrote that political campaigns are often referred to with a traditionally masculine vocabulary of "battles" or "wars" that need to be fought and won. She suggested, "Because politics and campaigns are rooted in

Having greater diversity among campaign leaders and people running for office helps to make elected officials more representative of the population.

THE STRENGTH OF GRASSROOTS MOVEMENTS

Chop down a tree's trunk and the whole tree dies. Kill a patch of grass and its root structure, called a rhizome, will continue to grow horizontally to form many new shoots.

In politics, a rhizomatic movement—or a grassroots movement—allows different groups of people to unite as a single force. Leadership is decentralized, meaning that there isn't a single leader running the show. This makes it difficult to stop a grassroots movement—even if a few strong leaders are silenced, there are many other leaders to take up the cause.

How do grassroots movements mobilize volunteers when they don't have a single organization making all the decisions? Here are a few strategies.

Build relationships: In a paper about building grassroots leaders published by NYU Wagner, community organizer Larry Ferlazzo said, "A group of people in a room that have no relationship with each other is a mob. A group of people in a room that have a relationship with each other is power." In other words, in a strong grassroots movement, activists and leaders must respect and listen to all potential allies.

Find new passionate leaders: The key to a successful grassroots movement is ensuring that there isn't just one leader. Many leaders must join the movement, even if their interests and passions are slightly different from other leaders in the group. In fact, it's often their differences that make the entire rhizomatic movement stronger.

Partner with other grassroots organizations: United grassroots movements rely on partnership. The People for Bernie Sanders, for example, was a movement that supported Senator Bernie Sanders before he announced his candidacy for US president in 2015. Made up of many different grassroots organizations, each group functioned independently, but they fought together for a single purpose—to help get Sanders elected. Sanders did not win the election, but his campaign became recognized for the attention it received due to its grassroots efforts.

masculinity and have long been the territory solely of men, women enter electoral politics as deviations from the norm."

Further, Dittmar suggested that "loosening the hold of traditional gender stereotypes—where candidacy for public office has been aligned with expectations about masculine strength—will enlarge the pool of willing candidates and help reduce women's underrepresentation in U.S. politics."

Leadership takes many forms, but when that leadership reflects a wider diversity of people, a campaign surely will attract a larger diversity of volunteers, and, eventually, voters. For example, after Democratic hopeful Hillary Clinton won the popular vote but narrowly lost the electoral vote for president in 2016, droves of women flocked to politics to help female politicians get elected in future campaigns.

RECRUIT, RECRUIT, RECRUIT!

If finding a great campaign manager is the first task of a budding campaign, recruiting volunteers comes in at a close second on the list of priorities. It can feel daunting to find volunteers. The easiest strategy might be to ask friends, family, or even teachers to join the ranks of volunteers, but the goal is to enlist as many members of a community as possible.

Whether handing out free lemonade at a farmer's market or setting up booths in a school cafeteria, a volunteer fair is a great way to share information about candidates.

LEADING A VOLUNTEER FAIR

Hosting a volunteer fair is a great way to attract people to a cause. Schools will often allow industrious, politically minded students to plan and execute a fair, provided there isn't any hate speech and that the interests of many students are met. For example, if there were a school election, a volunteer fair might be held in the gym or lunchroom and have different booths set up where each campaign could share information about their candidates and try to entice people to join up as volunteers.

If a school won't hold a fair, then it's time to think outside of the box. Ask the local farmer's market if you can set up a stand to hand out free lemonade while getting people to sign up as volunteers, or connect with nonprofits in the area to ask their advice— some nonprofits may even have their own upcoming volunteer fairs to partner with.

RAISING YOUR VOICE ON SOCIAL MEDIA

Most people enjoy being a part of a group, and social media platforms provide an easy way to create groups. By 2021, Statista estimates that there will be 3.2 billion social media users. When used wisely, social media can really help with volunteer recruitment efforts.

On Facebook, for example, pages can be made specifically for finding volunteers. Let's say, just hypothetically, that a campaign called "My Grandpa for Governor" needs to find volunteers. Starting a Facebook page titled "The People for My Grandpa for Governor" might attract a wider group of people than just friends and family. Adding photos of the candidate (in this case, perhaps, a smiling grandpa sitting in a rocking chair) and sharing great reasons why people would want to get involved (in this case, perhaps, "Rockin' Politics Since the 1950s") might also encourage potential volunteers to share news about the page with their friends.

CHAPTER THREE

HOW TO MANAGE VOLUNTEERS

Some grassroots organizations in the United States have tens of thousands of members. Now, imagine if none of those volunteers were provided with training or told the rules of the organization. It would be chaos! Therefore, having at least some basic rules, guidelines, and common goals are important. Volunteers should be provided guidance about what to do and when to do it.

HOW TO KEEP VOLUNTEERS ONCE YOU'VE GOT THEM

Finding volunteers is just half the battle. Once they sign on, it's important to focus on keeping them. There are a few different strategies for keeping volunteers enthusiastic and engaged.

PROVIDE GREAT TRAINING AND SUPERVISION

No one wants to work for a mediocre campaign. Good volunteer training not only provides volunteers with information that will help them as they assume their new roles, it also conveys a strong sense of professionalism. In addition, training helps volunteers feel like part of a team and allows them to know the same information

Providing training to volunteers will help them feel like important members of the team and will ensure they know what to do in their assigned roles.

about candidates as all of the other volunteers. Here are a couple of tips that will help.

Don't assume everyone learns the same way: Some people are visual learners, while others take in information by either reading or hearing it. Therefore, training should always include tools and materials that can be listened to, read, and watched. These materials should repeat some of the same information and might include written packets of information, videos, and conversations.

Don't let people burn out: There's nothing wrong with working hard but asking volunteers to work unusually long hours may cause them to burn out or get exhausted. It may also cause them to feel "used" by the campaign or resentful of the people in the campaign who are directing them to work. During training, volunteers should be provided with clear direction, including how many hours they are expected to work, when and if meals will be provided, and whom they should speak with if they start to feel stressed or burned out.

Be kind and thoughtful: Since volunteers are not paid in money, they should at least be paid in kindness. Providing volunteers with a comfortable place to work, logging their hours to make sure they're not overworked, and providing meals on the occasional long day all go a long way toward helping volunteers feel appreciated.

Check in with volunteers regularly: This means asking volunteers how they feel about the work they're being given and if they have any feedback for the campaign. This is a crucial part of supervising volunteers.

TEAMWORK WITH A CAPITAL "T"

There's an old saying that goes, "Teamwork makes the dream work." This is certainly true of volunteer teams: fostering a strong, supportive, caring campaign culture builds better teams.

Over time, the best teams in the world start to feel like families. In an article for *Inc.*, Carmine Gallo writes about how although Duke University's men's basketball team has certain "star" players, coach Mike Krzyzewski ensures that all of his basketball players feel as though they are "future superstars." Gallo writes, "Together as a team, they feel unstoppable—and that's by design."

The most effective political campaign managers also know that they need to make each volunteer feel like a superstar. They strive to create an environment that helps volunteers feel like one big, happy family. Volunteers often work together for months on the campaign trail, going to the same events, parties, and rallies. Teamwork is what drives all of these activities, and the excitement people share with one another inspires new volunteers to join.

Help every volunteer feel like a superstar by engaging them in "get to know you" activities such as icebreakers and games.

CAMPAIGNS SHOULD BE FUN!

Even in a high-stakes environment like a political campaign, people want to have fun. From making goal trackers to organizing "get to know you" events, here are a few easy ways to engage volunteers working on a campaign.

Icebreakers: Joining a campaign as a volunteer can feel intimidating. Icebreakers are little games that allow people to get to know each other and lighten the mood. A simple icebreaker is just to go around the room and ask people to share the story of how they got their name. Another icebreaker is to ask people to share their favorite color, food, or movie and then to go around the room trying to remember each person's favorite things.

Goal trackers: A little friendly competition often makes a political campaign more exciting. For instance, volunteers can be divided into two groups and given the challenge of calling the most voters. The winning team gets a pizza.

Fashion designer contest: Why not take things up a notch by having a fashion contest for volunteers? Print out sheets of paper with an empty cutout of a T-shirt (front and back), and ask people to design a T-shirt that relates to the campaign. The winning design can be made into real T-shirts that can be sold along the campaign trail. This contest can also be opened up to the community.

Theme days: Just as schools have "twins day" (when students dress as twins) or "wild hair day" (when students do their hair in outrageous styles), political campaigns can also have theme days. If the campaign has an office, it might be fun to have everyone show up one day wearing the same color. Or you can organize something as simple as "donut day," which is just what it sounds like!

TYPICAL VOLUNTEER JOBS

Many people have no clue what they're in for when they sign up to volunteer for a political campaign. The good news is that working on a campaign is often different every single day, making the time go by quickly. There are, however, a handful of typical "jobs" that many campaign volunteers will be asked to assume.

GETTING OUT INTO THE NEIGHBORHOOD

Walking and talking—that, in a nutshell, sums up the job of canvassing. Perhaps a slightly longer job description for a canvasser includes talking with pedestrians on the street or knocking door-to-door to engage with potential voters.

Oftentimes, canvassers carry clipboards and will gather signatures for various petitions or ask people to sign up as campaign volunteers. Some canvassing events are especially exciting. For example, in early 2019, Voter Choice Massachusetts let the wider online

Walking and talking, or canvassing, is a way to interact fact-to-face with potential voters and even get people to sign up as volunteers with a campaign.

community know about an opportunity to canvass at something called "Senator Elizabeth Warren's Announcement Event." A page on the organization's website said, "Elizabeth Warren is hosting an event to make a 'big announcement,'" making people wonder if she was going to run for president. Warren did, in fact, announce her run as a Democratic presidential candidate, which must have made the event thrilling for any volunteer in the audience.

Although not all canvassing jobs are as exciting as a senator announcing she's running for president, they are great gigs for personable volunteers who enjoy meeting new people, getting a little exercise, and being outdoors.

PHONE BANKS

During Republican president George W. Bush's 2004 run for a second term as president, his campaign devoted half a million dollars to phone banks. Although that might seem like a lot of money just to make some phone calls, phone banks, which essentially involve volunteers calling people to talk with them about a particular candidate or ask if they will be heading to the voter polls, are an effective piece of the campaigning pie.

Similar to canvassing, phone banks give volunteers the opportunity to get to know people in the community. They can record the people who say they plan on voting for a candidate, people who say they won't, and, most importantly, they can get a sense of people who are still on the fence about whom they will vote

A large number of Americans still have landlines, and campaigns can use this fact to their advantage by using phone banks to reach potential voters.

for. This allows volunteers to then circle back to try to convince them to vote for their candidates or even send canvassers to their homes to try to make a face-to-face appeal.

Although it might seem like most people are using only cell phones these days, there are still a surprisingly large number of Americans who have landlines (phones that can be used only in the home or at a business). In fact, according to the US Centers for Disease Control and Prevention National Health Information Survey, about 42.8 percent of Americans still used landlines in

2017—definitely a high enough percentage of potential voters to use phone banks!

DATA ENTRY

For people who don't want to engage with potential voters, data entry is the perfect job as a volunteer on a political campaign. Basically, the job involves taking information about the campaign or voters and entering it into a database.

Data entry is known for being a tedious job, but it shouldn't be thankless. In other words, the campaign and volunteer managers should make sure to set aside plenty of time for volunteers who are assisting with data entry to interact with others working on the campaign.

Some data entry jobs even allow volunteers to head out into the community. According to Ben Holse, senior account manager for the Campaign Workshop, "There are a number of campaign tools now available that can help reduce the amount of data that you have to enter at the end of the day. The technology exists for canvassers to enter data on their smartphones or tablets while they are canvassing."

CHAPTER FOUR

COMMUNITY EVENTS

Getting out in front of the community is a vital part of all campaigns. Shaking hands, getting to know neighbors, listening to concerns, and sharing views are all things that candidates should get comfortable with pretty quickly. The best campaigns find creative ways to do this work—inspiring voters can include many different sorts of community events!

FUNDRAISING EVENTS

Campaigns often need money—sometimes a lot of money—to help get a candidate elected. One of the best ways for a political campaign to make money is by organizing not just one but many events for the community. In 2016, Bernie Sanders's campaign organized countless grassroots events across the United States. Some events attracted hundreds of people, while others were attended by only a few people. According to an article in ABC News, events "were held in bars, backyards, and basements." Some

Political candidates can raise money in a number of ways, from holding intimate fundraisers in people's homes to hosting huge events for hundreds of people.

events attracted hundreds of people, but the number of people who RSVP'd for other events was as low as four. This just goes to show that, in a grassroots campaign, it's not always necessary to hold the biggest, grandest event—even a pizza party in somebody's living room can inspire people to donate money to help elect a favorite candidate.

FROM THE COMFORT OF YOUR OWN HOME

Planning a fundraiser at home is a great way to solicit donations from the community. First, it's vital to set a fundraising goal. Goal setting not only helps the organizers of the fundraisers, but it also inspires people to donate to try to reach the goal.

It's also important to figure out before the event how food, drinks, and other items for the fundraiser will be paid for. Many people who host fundraisers in their homes will donate their own funds to cover expenses, but asking members of the community to contribute is also an option. Funds raised during the event can also cover expenses, but this should be decided in advance for the sake of being transparent.

BUSINESS VENUES

Using a business venue to hold larger fundraising events is a great idea. Schools, churches, and community centers will often donate the space, although renting venues is also an option.

It's helpful to know in advance how many people will attend an event by asking people to RSVP. Carefully recording RSVPs also helps fundraiser planners follow up with event-goers after an event to thank them for attending and potentially invite them to participate in future events or fundraising endeavors.

Before hosting a fundraising event, consider whether it will be a free or ticketed event. If the latter, the cost of tickets shouldn't exceed what people can actually afford. For example, if the event is held for teenagers, a ticket might be less than if the event is primarily for working adults.

SILENT AUCTIONS, CONCERTS, AND PERFORMANCES

Fundraising possibilities are endless. Musical concerts and other performances are always fun, and they can be planned by people of all ages and talents. When planning an event, first take the temperature of the community and try to think outside of the box. For example, if a particular community is known for having a beautiful lake, consider having an ice cream social or beach party fundraiser in the summer, or an ice-skating event in the winter.

Silent auctions can yield big rewards for a fundraiser. These events collect items from members of the community and then give them to the person who bids the highest

Performances, concerts, and silent auctions are fantastic ways to fundraise for a campaign, although it's also good to think outside the box.

DON'T FORGET ONLINE FUNDRAISING

The internet forever changed political fundraising. These days, online fundraising, or crowdfunding, events are just as important as on-the-ground events, and they often yield more donations. President Barack Obama's 2012 campaign, for example, brought in $1.1 billion through fundraising efforts. About half of this amount—$525 million—was through online fundraising.

Whereas traditional fundraising often focuses on raising large amounts of money from a small number of people, online fundraising collects small donations from many people. Below are a couple of user-friendly strategies for raising money over the internet.

Email campaigns: According to a 2018 study by the Radicati Group, more than 3.8 billion people use email—that's more than half of all humans! Therefore, it makes sense to use email platforms to develop fundraising campaigns. Online platforms such as Constant Contact and Mailchimp provide email templates to create campaigns, and they can save separate lists of potential donors and people who have already donated.

Crowdfunding sites: Crowdfunding is big business. According to a 2018 report by Statista, $17.2 billion is raised annually through online community-pooled funding in North America alone. There are about 375 online crowdfunding platforms, many of which make it easy to start campaigns. Kickstarter, Indiegogo, and GoFundme are some popular crowdfunding sites. Using these platforms, people can contribute small amounts of money in return for some sort of reward or just out of the goodness of their hearts.

Crowdfunding helps ensure that elections aren't just decided by wealthy people. In a 2014 article in Alliance magazine, Breanna DiGiammarino from Indiegogo said, "Crowdfunding democratizes fundraising and empowers citizens to develop innovative solutions and feel the pride of participating together to make things happen within their local communities or across an ocean."

amount of money. They are called silent because people mark their bids on a piece of paper rather than announcing their bids out loud. Auctions are also a time to get creative. For example, artists can donate art work, local businesses can donate gift cards or services, and gyms can donate memberships.

PLAN EVENTS TO TALK ABOUT BIG IDEAS

While a campaign is nothing without its volunteers and supporters, it's also meaningless without its ideas. Therefore, it's really important to plan events that get candidates out into the public eye to share their ideas as often as possible.

FACING AN OPPONENT

Facing a political opponent during a debate is often a pivotal point in a campaign. For presidential elections, debates are publicized, televised events with millions of people watching. For school council, they might take place on a stage in front of a few classes. More than just an opportunity to hear candidates' opposing views, they also give potential voters a chance to see how each candidate deals with pressure—every facial gesture, shrug, and sigh is scrutinized. Shortly before the 2016 US presidential election, presidential historian Michael Beschloss told NBC News that debates "show us things about candidates that other venues do not,

A televised presidential debate made John F. Kennedy seem younger and cooler than his opponent, helping him to win the highest office in the United States: the presidency.

but they also sometimes overwhelm everything else we know about a candidate."

The first presidential debate in the United States was in 1960, and it helped contribute to Democrat John F. Kennedy's win for president over Republican vice president Richard Nixon. Television audiences saw a sweaty and pale Nixon next to the young, vigorous, and cool-as-a-cucumber Kennedy.

Of course, what audiences didn't know was that before the event, Kennedy had makeup applied to give his cheeks a healthy-looking glow and to prevent having a shiny face. Poor Nixon, however, not only refused the offer of makeup, he was also a little worse-for-wear after a recent hospital visit.

So what's the moral of the story? While looks shouldn't matter, giving the appearance of being healthy and ready to lead does matter. When campaigns plan debates, they should not only spend many hours prepping candidates by practicing how to answer various questions, they should also help candidates by ensuring they get a good night's sleep before the debate, as well as provide other tips for appearing rested and healthy in front of discerning audiences

ANSWERING QUESTIONS FIRED OFF BY THE PEOPLE

A town hall gives an opportunity for citizens to ask questions directly to candidates. A town hall might just showcase one candidate, or it might be used as a debate platform where two candidates can answer questions from the public.

During a town hall, candidates must demonstrate that they are mentally nimble, answering even the most difficult questions in a measured, smart manner. Oftentimes, the questions directed from community members border on personal, rather than just relating to policy, and they reveal a lot about candidates' deep-seated values. For example, when asked about his age (thirty-seven) at a town hall at the music festival SXSW in 2019, Democratic presidential hopeful Pete Buttigieg replied that it "allows me to communicate to the country a vision of what the country is going to look like in 2054—that's the year I'll get to the age of the current president. When you're personally preparing for what the world is going to look like, then it gives you a different sense of urgency."

Unfortunately, just as much as the town hall format can allow candidates a chance to provide glowing, personal answers, they can also shine a light on candidates' flaws if they aren't able to answer questions or if they get angry or too impassioned. This is why it's important for candidates to spend many hours practicing how they'd answer a myriad of questions ranging from personal to those about political policy.

MEET AND GREETS

Offering members of the community the opportunity to meet a candidate in person can leave a lasting first impression. These events allow time for handshakes, smiles, and person-to-person contact.

When scheduling meet and greets, it's important to choose the right location. A candidate for local sheriff might choose a park, while a mayoral candidate might flip some burgers outside a grocery store on a nice, spring day. Presidential candidates have conducted meet and greets anywhere from small diners to churches to homes.

A meet and greet is a perfect opportunity for volunteers working the campaign to pass out materials about the candidate and collect donations. Often a table will be set up so that members of the community can sign up for more information or to add their names to a mailing list. When campaigns have a large enough

Meet and greets are a way for political candidates to get to know potential voters and make a great first impression.

budget, meet and greets can make buttons or other campaign items to pass out.

Of course, candidates must mentally prepare themselves for meet and greets. Having a constant smile on one's face, answering back-to-back questions, and just being generally "on" for extended periods of time can feel exhausting, so it's important not to schedule meet and greets that last more than an hour or so.

CHAPTER FIVE

THE LAWS OF A CAMPAIGN

Laws are important for a society—without them, there wouldn't be repercussions for crimes. Political campaigns are also ruled by laws. In fact, a campaign could fail if it either doesn't understand campaign laws or chooses to ignore them.

WHO CAN AND CAN'T JOIN A CAMPAIGN?

Not everyone can join a political campaign. Knowing who can and can't join a campaign and who can and can't volunteer for a campaign is important. Officially, the Federal Election Commission (FEC) of the United States of America mandates that "an individual may volunteer personal services to a campaign without making a contribution as long as the individual is not compensated by anyone for the services." But there are a few other things to know.

PEOPLE OF ALL AGES

Although the voting age in the United States is eighteen, even minors can participate in political campaigns. In fact, young people make great volunteers. They can canvass, phone bank, help plan events, and take on other campaign jobs just as well as adults.

For some young people, a political campaign is their first foray into politics. Before deciding to side with one candidate over another, it's important to learn about all of the options. Pore over the websites of each candidate, watch their speeches on TV, and get to know the issues they feel strongly about. Most of all,

Even minors can participate in political campaigns by taking on various volunteer jobs. Find out how you can get involved by reading about the candidates in your area.

young people shouldn't feel obliged to volunteer for a candidate just because their parents or community support that person. It's better to consider whether a candidate's issues and beliefs mirror one's own. For young people, it's important to examine how candidates tackle issues that impact the lives of children, teens, and college students. How does a candidate, for example, deal with education, student loans, and teacher issues?

Once a young person has chosen a candidate, it's pretty easy to sign up as a volunteer. Websites often have sign-up sheets. Candidates may have a local office where volunteers can sign up. People can also contact Youth Service America, an organization that helps connect young people with volunteer opportunities.

Of course, for smaller campaigns—like ones developed for school elections—sometimes it's just as easy as tracking down the candidate in the hallway to say, "Hey, I'd like to volunteer for your campaign!"

FOREIGN NATIONALS

In the United States, special rules apply to foreign nationals who want to get involved in an election. For example, regulations implemented by the FEC "prohibit foreign nationals from directing, dictating, controlling, or directly or indirectly participating in the decision-making process of any person (such as a corporation, labor organization, political committee, or political organization) with regard to any election-related activities."

Basically, this is a fancy way of saying the laws governing non-Americans wanting to volunteer for a campaign are complicated. A good rule of thumb for foreign nationals—including undocumented immigrants—is to first speak with the political campaign they'd like to work with to ask how they may and may not contribute as a volunteer.

MONEY TALKS

Financially supporting a candidate is a great thing, but there are many rules about making contributions to political campaigns. Learning the laws about financial contributions is important, particularly as these laws can really impact communities.

WHO CAN'T CONTRIBUTE?

Just as there are laws for who can participate in a political campaign, there are also regulations dictating who may and may not contribute donations. Most individuals can make contributions to political party committees, but there are exceptions.

According to the FEC, foreign nationals are prohibited from "making any contribution or donation of money or other thing of value, or making any expenditure, independent expenditure, or disbursement in connection with any federal, state, or local election in the United States." In short, they're not allowed to give even a dollar to any campaign.

People under eighteen may make contributions, but only if they haven't been prompted to make their

CAMPAIGN FINANCE VIOLATIONS

In the United States, campaign finance laws regulate how much money in donations campaigns and political parties can receive from individuals or organizations. These laws should be understood by people making political contributions, but, most importantly, they must be followed by campaigns.

In 1971, the Federal Election Campaign Act (FECA) was signed into law. FECA has been amended many times to include further campaign finance restrictions. In 2002, it was amended to include hefty consequences for violating campaign finance laws. For example, people can go to prison for two years for violations over $10,000 and for up to five years for violations over $25,000. According to this law, any violation of over $2,000 in a year can be punishable.

In 2018, President Donald Trump's former lawyer, Michael Cohen, was sentenced to three years in prison for violating campaign finance laws.

contributions by anyone else. Adults may not make contributions on behalf of a minor without that minor knowing and agreeing to the donation. Additionally, funds can't be given to a minor for the purpose of making a donation.

HOW MUCH CAN PEOPLE CONTRIBUTE?

There are limits to how much money people can donate to campaigns. In 2019 to 2020, for example, an individual could contribute up to $2,800 per election to a candidate's committee, or up $5,000 per year to a PAC (political action committee) created for the purpose of raising and spending money to elect a particular candidate or defeat another candidate.

In addition to contributing money to individual candidates, people can give money to a political party. These amounts can typically be larger, ranging from $10,000 for local and state parties to tens of thousands of dollars for national political parties. The amounts people can donate change regularly, so it's important to check FEC regulations on the commission's website, www.fec.gov, before making larger donations.

POLITICS IS FOR EVERYONE!

Politics aren't just for politicians. Candidates campaign for public office, but they should always be fighting for the interests of their constituents—the people who voted for them. Therefore, it's a big mistake for a political campaign to ignore the interests of people.

Working on or volunteering with a political campaign allows anyone and everyone to get involved in politics. Aside from helping to create change, it's a great way to make new friends!

They should find out what their constituents care about well before Election Day.

Anyone can get involved in politics. Working on a campaign can be a deeply rewarding experience. Volunteering offers people of all ages and from all walks of life the opportunity to meet others who share their interests, but, more importantly, it lets them better understand the inner workings of the political systems that so deeply impact their daily lives.

campaign finance laws Special laws that regulate how money is used in elections.

candidate A person seeking to be elected to a political office.

canvassing A form of face-to-face contact with potential voters or other members of the community, whereby volunteers or candidates go door to door to engage people.

census A process of officially counting a population.

crowdfunding A way to raise small amounts of money from many people, often by using online fundraising tools and platforms.

debate A process in which political candidates state their opinions on issues and argue with their opponents in a public space.

focus group A means of understanding public opinion on an issue by having a small, often diverse group of people discuss the issue.

foreign national A person who is neither a citizen nor a legal permanent resident of the country where she or he lives.

grassroots movement A decentralized movement without a single leader; multiple groups coming together to fight for a single cause.

meet and greet An event where a political candidate gets to meet and speak with the public, often informally.

phone bank Making phone calls to connect with voters and encourage them to vote.

political contribution A donation made to a political party or candidate.

poll The process of surveying an often random group of people to find out their opinions about particular issues.

rhizome An underground system of plant stems that grows horizontally rather than vertically, sending out a multitude of new shoots.

town hall An event at which a political candidate answers questions asked directly by members of the community.

volunteer A person who willingly undertakes a service without payment.

vote The act of choosing one political candidate over all others, typically by marking a ballot.

US Constitution A document signed in 1787 that established the United States of America's national government and primary laws.

Canada Service Corps
Website: https://www.canada.ca/en/services/youth
/canada-service-corps.html
Facebook and Instagram: @LeadersToday
Twitter: @Jobs_Emplois
Launched in 2018, the Canada Service Corps is a large
platform funded by the government of Canada that
connects youth to volunteer opportunities across
Canada's provinces.

Center for Information & Research on Civic Learning
and Engagement (CIRCLE)
Jonathan M. Tisch College of Civic Life
Tufts University
Lincoln Filene Hall
10 Upper Campus Road
Medford, MA 02155
(617) 627-3453
Website: http://civicyouth.org
Facebook: @Center-for-Information-Research-on-Civic
-Learning-and-Engagement-CIRCLE
Twitter: @CivicYouth
CIRCLE helps increase civic engagement of young
people and works to change policy that affects
marginalized youth.

Emily's List
1800 M Street NW, Suite 375N
Washington, DC 20036
(202) 326-1400
Website: https://www.emilyslist.org

Facebook and Twitter: @EmilysList
Instagram: @Emilys_List
Emily's List is an organization that helps elect
    progressive women to political office.

Federal Election Commission of the United States of
    America
1050 First Street NE
Washington, DC 20463
(800) 424-9530
Website: https://www.fec.gov
Twitter: @FEC
This federal commission was developed to regulate
    and provide information about the campaign finance
    process in the United States.

Rock the Vote
1440 G Street NW
Washington, DC 20005
(202) 719-9910
Website: https://www.rockthevote.org
Facebook, Instagram, and Twitter: @rockthevote
Rock the Vote is a nonpartisan and progressive
    nonprofit organization that uses music, pop culture,
    and art to motivate young people to get involved in
    politics, build their political power, and make voting
    work for everyone.

Volunteer Canada
309 Cooper Street, Suite 201
Ottawa, ON K2P0G5

Canada
(613) 231-4371
Website: https://volunteer.ca
Facebook and Twitter: @VolunteerCanada
Established in 1977, Volunteer Canada works to increase
    the quantity and quality of volunteer experiences. The
    organization partners with other volunteer centers
    and nonprofit organizations to reach out to as many
    potential volunteers as possible.

Youth Service America (YSA)
1050 Connecticut Avenue NW, Room 65525
Washington, DC 20036
(202) 296-2992
Website: https://ysa.org/vote
Facebook: @youthserviceamerica
Instagram and Twitter: @youthservice
Youth Service America (YSA) helps increase the
    number and quality of volunteer opportunities for
    young people at thousands of organizations.

Baumgardner, Jennifer, and Amy Richards. *Grassroots: A Field Guide for Feminist Activism*. New York, NY: Farrar, Straus, and Giroux, 2013.

Bond, Becky, and Zack Exley. *Rules for Revolutionaries: How Big Organizing Could Change Everything*. White River Junction, VT: Chelsea Green Publishing, 2017.

Klobuchar, Amy. *Nevertheless, We Persisted: 48 Voices of Defiance, Strength, and Courage*. New York, NY: Penguin Random House, 2018.

Lewis, Barbara A., and Michelle Lee. *The Kid's Guide to Service Projects: Over 500 Service Ideas for Young People Who Want to Make a Difference*. Minneapolis, MN: Free Spirit Publishing, 2009.

Lowery, Lynda Blackmon, et al. *Turning 15 on the Road to Freedom: My Story of the 1965 Selma Voting Rights March*. New York, NY: Penguin Random House, 2016.

Martin, Bobi. *What Are Elections?* New York, NY: Rosen Publishing, 2016.

Martin, Courtney E. *Do It Anyway: The New Generation of Activists*. Boston, MA: Beacon Press, 2010.

Sanders, Bernie. *Where We Go from Here: Two Years in the Resistance*. New York, NY: St. Martin's Press, 2018.

Westley, Frances, et al. *Getting to Maybe: How the World Is Changed*. Toronto, ON: Vintage Canada, 2011.

BIBLIOGRAPHY

Abramson, Alana, and Maryalice Parks. "Bernie Sanders Claims 100,000 Involved in Mega-Grassroots Event." ABC News, July 29, 2015. https://abcnews.go.com /US/bernie-sanders-claims-100000-involved-mega -grassroots-event/story?id=32770278.

Bailey, Holly. "Steve Schmidt: The Man Behind McCain." *Newsweek*, October 10, 2008. https://www.newsweek .com/steve-schmidt-man-behind-mccain-92215.

Blumberg, Stephen J., and Julian V. "Wireless Substitution: Early Release of Estimates from the National Health Interview Survey, July–December 2017." National Center for Health Statistics. Retrieved April 18, 2019. https://www.cdc.gov/nchs/data/nhis /earlyrelease/wireless201806.pdf.

Buckley, Tamara, and Jonathan Walters. "Building Community Power by Building Grassroots Leaders: Sacramento Valley Organizing Committee (SVOC)." The Electronic Hallway, NYU Wagner. Retrieved July 28, 2019. https://wagner.nyu.edu/files/leadership /SacramentoValleyOrganizingCommunity.pdf.

Contreras, Natalia E. "Top 5 Takeaways from Pete Buttigieg's CNN Town Hall at SXSW." Indy Star, March 10, 2019. https://www.indystar.com/story /news/2019/03/10/pete-buttigieg-sxsw-top-5 -takeaways-cnn-town-hall/3125486002.

DeSilver, Drew. "U.S. Trails Most Developed Countries in Voter Turnout." Pew Research Center, May 21, 2018. https://www.pewresearch.org/fact-tank/2018/05/21/u-s -voter-turnout-trails-most-developed-countries.

Dittmar, Kelly. "How Views About Gender Shape U.S. Election Campaigns." Scholars Strategy Network,

January 7, 2015. https://scholars.org/brief/how-views
-about-gender-shape-us-election-campaigns.

Dittmar, Kelly. *Navigating Gendered Terrain: Stereotypes
and Strategy in Political Campaigns.* Philadelphia, PA:
Temple University Press, 2015.

Federal Election Committee of the United States of
America. Retrieved February 17, 2019. https://www
.fec.gov.

Gallo, Carmine. "Duke Basketball's Coach K Uses a
Powerful Communication Tactic to Build and Motivate
Winning Teams." *Inc.*, March 21, 2019. https://www.inc
.com/carmine-gallo/duke-basketballs-coach-k-uses
-a-powerful-communication-tactic-to-build-motivate
-winning-teams.html.

Gilder Lehrman Collection. "Wide-Awake Election of 1860
Campaign Ribbon." Retrieved March 1, 2019. https://
www.gilderlehrman.org/content/wide-awake-election
-1860-campaign-ribbon.

Goodman, Jordi, Ashley Wennerstrom, and Benjamin
Springgate. *Participatory and Social Media to Engage
Youth: From the Obama Campaign to Public Health
Practice. Ethnicity & Disease* 2011 Summer; 21 (3 0 1):
S1–94-9.

Harris, Chris. "Super Tuesday Youth Voter Turnout Triples,
Quadruples in Some States." MTV.com, February 6,
2008. http://www.mtv.com/news/1581027/super
-tuesday-youth-voter-turnout-triples-quadruples-in
-some-states.

Holse, Ben. "Political Organizers Top Tips for Campaign
Data Entry." *The Campaign Workshop Blog*, June 19,
2013. https://www.thecampaignworkshop.com
/political-organizers-top-tips-campaign-data-entry-tcw.

Howard, Adam. "10 Presidential Debates That Actually Made an Impact." The Campaign Workshop, September 25, 2016. https://www.thecampaignworkshop.com/political-organizers-top-tips-campaign-data-entry-tcw.

Kuraishi, Mari. "From Crowdfunding to Crowdsourcing." *Alliance*, June 1, 2014. https://www.alliancemagazine.org/analysis/from-crowdfunding-to-crowdsourcing.

McMillan, Graeme. "Harvey Dent Wants Your Vote, Half Your Suit." Gizmodo, March 10, 2008. https://io9.gizmodo.com/harvey-dent-wants-your-vote-half-your-suit-365691.

Parks, Maryalice. "Women Are Running for Office in Historic Numbers. Here Are 10 Female Candidates to Watch." ABC News, November 6, 2018. https://abcnews.go.com/GMA/News/women-running-office-historic-numbers-10-female-candidates/story?id=58079170.

Radicati Group, Inc., The. "Email Statistics Report, 2018-2022." March 2018. https://www.radicati.com/wp/wp-content/uploads/2017/12/Email-Statistics-Report-2018-2022-Executive-Summary.pdf.

Statista. "Number of Social Media Users Worldwide from 2010 to 2021 (in Billions)." Retrieved March 20, 2019. https://www.statista.com/statistics/278414/number-of-worldwide-social-network-users.

United States Census Bureau. "U.S. and World Population Clock." Retrieved April 2, 2019. https://www.census.gov/popclock.

Voter Choice Massachusetts. "Canvass at Elizabeth Warren's Announcement Event." Retrieved March 1, 2019. https://www.voterchoicema.org/canvass_at_elizabeth_warren_s_announcement_event.

ABOUT THE AUTHOR

Melissa Banigan is the founder and CEO of Advice Project Media, a nonprofit that offers journalism training for youth and women around the world. An author and educator, she has taught and lectured about gender equality, feminism, and teen rights in the United States, Cameroon, Peru, and Guadeloupe. Also a multimedia journalist, Banigan has bylines in many national and international publications, including the *Washington Post*, CNN, NPR, and the BBC. Her first book, *Coping with Teen Pregnancy* (Rosen Publishing), was released in January 2019.

PHOTO CREDITS

Cover Rafal Rodzoch/Caiaimage/Getty Images; pp. 4–5 (background graphics) weerawan/iStock/Getty Images; p. 5 Private Collection/Photo © Don Troiani/Bridgeman Images; p. 9 H. Mark Weidman Photography/Alamy Stock Photo; p. 11 Monkey Business Images/Shutterstock.com; p. 13 Joshua Rainey Photography/Shutterstock.com; p. 16 Paul J. Richards/AFP/Getty Images; p. 19 Win McNamee/Getty Images; p. 20 NY Daily News Archive/Getty Images; p. 21 Ethan Miller/Getty Images; p. 24 Ariel Skelley/DigitalVision/Getty Images; p. 27 Joshua Lott/Getty Images; p. 29 Tom Williams/CQ Roll Call/Getty Images; p. 31 Jessica McGowan/Getty Images; p. 33 Jim Watson/AFP/Getty Images; p. 36 Andrew Cline/Shutterstock.com; p. 38 Drew Anthony Smith/Getty Images; p. 41 Bettmann/Getty Images; p. 44 Bloomberg/Getty Images; p. 46 Milkovasa/Shutterstock.com; p. 49 Eduardo Munoz Alvarez/Getty Images; p. 51 © AP Images; additional graphic elements moodboard - Mike Watson Images/Brand X Pictures/Getty Images (chapter opener backgrounds), Maksim M/Shutterstock.com (fists).

Design: Michael Moy; Editor: Rachel Aimee; Photo Researcher: Nicole DiMella